The Thursday Club

Animal Poems

Gordon Snell has written more than twenty books
for children, many of them in verse. He is also the author
of plays, song lyrics and opera librettoes performed
on stage, radio and television. He is married to
the writer Maeve Binchy.

The Thursday Club

Club

Animal Poems

Gordon Snell

Illustrated by Anthony Flintoft

Dolphin

First published in Great Britain in 2000
as a Dolphin Paperback
by Orion Children's Books
a division of the Orion Publishing Group Ltd
Orion House
5 Upper St Martin's Lane
London WC2 9EA

Text © Gordon Snell 2000
Illustrations © Anthony Flintoft 2000

The right of Gordon Snell and Anthony Flintoft to be identified as author and illustrator
of this work has been asserted.

A catalogue record for this book is available from the British Library.

These tales by animals related,
To Maeve with love are dedicated.

Contents

Look at the end of each section to
find the answers to the quiz poems!

Stories in the Forest

If you wander in the forest
On a Thursday, you will find
Gathered in a great big circle
Animals of every kind.

There the Thursday Club is meeting:
Happily they pass the time
Telling stories to each other,
Telling stories all in rhyme.
Riddles they will also tell,
Tongue twisters and games as well.

There to choose the storytellers
Sits Big Bill, the woolly dog.
Each of them when they are chosen
Comes and stands upon a log.

The First Thursday

Big Bill now will make the choice
In his deep, melodious voice...

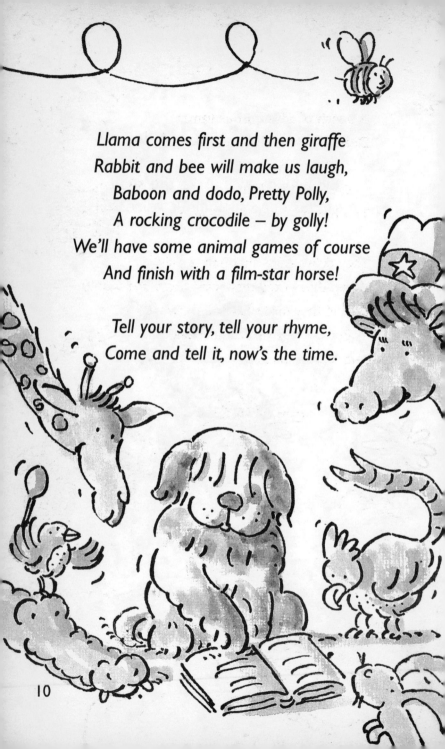

Llama comes first and then giraffe
Rabbit and bee will make us laugh,
Baboon and dodo, Pretty Polly,
A rocking crocodile – by golly!
We'll have some animal games of course
And finish with a film-star horse!

Tell your story, tell your rhyme,
Come and tell it, now's the time.

The Llamas' Holiday

A bunch of adventurous llamas
Dressed up in bright coloured pyjamas
    And set off one night
    On a holiday flight
To a beach in the balmy Bahamas.

They didn't enjoy themselves fully:
When they swam they were heavy and woolly –
    And they might have all drowned,
    But the lifeguard came round
And hoisted them out with a pulley!

The Giraffe Who Played I-Spy

The giraffe said, "I
Am as high as the sky.
I always win when we play I-SPY
Because my little eye
Is up so high."

Then, My-Oh-My!
A cloud came by –
The giraffe saw nothing when they played I-Spy
Because her little eye
Was up so high.

So she started to cry
Up there in the sky
Which caught the eye of a busybody fly
Just passing by
Up there in the sky.

The fly said, "Hi!
No need to cry –
The world's a lottery, so say I.
Some crawl, some fly,
Some live, some die!"

The giraffe said, "Why
Should I even reply?
Your words didn't help when you saw me cry
So I'll say goodbye . . ."
Then she ate that fly!

Rita the Rabbit

A rabbit called Rita was reckless and bold:
One day she fulfilled her mother's worst fears.
She said to her: "Mum, I am seven weeks old
And I think it's high time I was piercing my ears."

"No, no! I won't let you!" Her mother was shocked.
"Oh Rita, just think what the neighbours will say.
They'll stick up their noses, and I shall be mocked
For not stopping my daughter from having her way."

Rita's smile was as sweet as a bouquet of roses,
But to her such opinions just didn't make sense.
She borrowed some rings off the local bulls' noses
And then pierced her ears with barbed wire from a fence.

Her young friends admired her, but not so the neighbours!
And her mother wept tears at the rings she saw dangling.
But Rita enjoyed the results of her labours
As she heard her new jewellery jingling and jangling.

That night round the burrow a fox came a-creeping:
The scent of a rabbit had instant appeal.
He thought he would seize one while they were all sleeping
And take it off home and enjoy a good meal.

Just then Rita woke up, and poked her head out –
As the fox went to seize her, the silence was shattered:
When she pricked up her ears, the rings moved about,
And with jangling noises they clashed and they clattered.

The fox ran – he thought he'd set off an alarm,
And that people with guns would be after him soon.
The rabbits said: "Rita, you've saved us from harm
And you've shown that pierced ears can be truly a boon!"

The Bumblebee's Buzz

The bumblebee buzzes around
    BUZZ, BUZZ!
And look what the bumblebee found
    BUZZ, BUZZ!
A sack full of money
All covered in honey:
One hundred ten-p's and a pound
    BUZZ, BUZZ!

The bumblebee spent the whole lot
    BUZZ, BUZZ!
On a car and a house and a yacht,
    BUZZ, BUZZ!
A truck full of dates
And a pair of gold skates
And a hundred jam-tarts in a pot
    BUZZ, BUZZ!

The Baboon's Lament

Baboon, Baboon,
Under the moon,
Why do you sing such a gloomy tune?

I weep for the sun that shone so bright
And now has gone, and left us in night,
And left us in night so dark and black –
And how do we know it will ever come back?

No wonder I sing such a gloomy tune –
Baboon, Baboon,
Under the moon.

Baboon, Baboon,
In the afternoon,
It's time to be singing a cheerful tune.

For the sun has come and the sky is bright
And we've said goodbye to the dark of night.
Yes, it's here for now, and I can't complain –
But how do we know it won't leave us again?

That's why I can't sing a cheerful tune –
Baboon, Baboon,
In the afternoon.

Baboon, Baboon,
I can firmly say
You *enjoy* being gloomy by night or day!

So go on singing your gloomy tune
In May, December, July or June,
In the day or the night or the afternoon –
By the sun or the moon,
Baboon, Baboon!

19

The Dodo's Ode

A dodo one day came along
And said to the marvelling throng:
    "No wonder you blinked,
    For you thought me extinct –
But *I'm* here to prove you are wrong!"

Pretty Polly's Tongue Twister

Pretty Polly's pretty pally
With the parrots in the valley.
But Polly likes to dilly-dally
So she'll never win the Rally!

The Crocodile's Rock

A sparrow by the River Nile
Said boldly to a crocodile:
"Your teeth, as everyone agrees,
Are just as white as piano keys,
And if I tap them with this spoon
I'll bet you I can play a tune.
You'll soon be known, both near and far,
As Rocking Croc, the concert star!"

The crocodile, who liked applause,
Then promptly opened wide his jaws.
The sparrow hopped in straight away
And merrily began to play.
TAP-TAP! TAP-TAP! Each tooth he smote
Resounded with a different note.
But then – oh dear, the thought is chilling –
He hit a tooth that needed filling!

The crocodile cried out in pain
And quickly shut his jaws again,
And as those teeth together snapped
The sparrow found that he was trapped.
What if the croc began to munch,
Deciding it was time for lunch?

The sparrow with his wing-tips tried
Tickling the mouth he was inside
And sure enough, he soon was pleased
To find the crocodile had sneezed.
The jaws, wide open, went AAAH-CHOO!
And out the little sparrow flew.

He said: "That's put a stop, I fear,
To any musical career.
I did my best – and maybe, later,
I'll try to play the alligator!"

Animal Games

And now it is time for the Animal Games –
We give you the clues and you find out the names!

My First is a creature that's famed for its hump
My Second has horns and knows well how to jump.
My Third is a bird with a beautiful trill
My Fourth is an insect that lives in a hill.
My Fifth dwells in sewers where it scuttles and squeaks
My Sixth lives in Tibet, on mountainous peaks.

When you know them, then take the first letter of each
And put them together, the answer to reach.

The Star-Struck Horse

There was a horse called Glorious Grace
Who came in first in every race –
And yet in spite of all her fame
She didn't like the racing game.

Grace was determined, if she could,
To be a star in Hollywood.
In Wild West movies she'd do battle
And with the cowboys herd the cattle.

When next the winning-post was near
Then Grace began to buck and rear
And on hind-legs began to prance –
The jockey hadn't got a chance!

The trainer's shouts she didn't heed –
She planned to start a great stampede!
She neighed: "Hey, pardner, don't ya reckon
You-all can feel the Wild West beckon?"

The other horses all agreed
And soon they followed Grace's lead.
They bucked and reared and pranced around,
While jockeys sprawled upon the ground.

Then Grace led each and every horse
Over the fence around the course
And off they galloped, far and wide
Away into the countryside.

For days they roamed and did their best
To imitate the old Wild West:
They'd hunt for those who broke the law
And round up every cow they saw.

The trainers went and brought them back
To run again around the track;
But soon the story got about
Of how the horses all broke out.

And finally a film was made
About the Wild West games they played
And who was chosen as the horse
To be the star? Well, GRACE, of course!

Let's all clap our fins and claws,
Our wings, our hooves, our furry paws!
Here next week in sun or rain
The Thursday Club will meet again.

Page 24: Animal Games
Camel-Antelope-Nightingale-Ant-Rat-Yak = CANARY

The Second Thursday

Thursday's here, so shout HOORAY!
What stories will we have today?

Pony and octopus will start
Snow goose and zebra play their part
The bat flies in, then we've some puzzles,
A seal plays and a pelican guzzles.
Hamster and aardvark, slug as well –
Last, ravens have a tale to tell.

Tell your story, tell your rhyme,
Come and tell it, now's the time.

The Pony's Rhyme

There once was a pony
Called Tony Maloney
His tail it was long
And his back it was bony.

He once had a crony
Did Tony Maloney
Who moaned and who groaned
That the path was too stony.

"You're talking bolaney,"
Said Tony Maloney,
"Watch me roll on the ground
And I'll show you're a phoney!"

The Octopus's Eightsome Reel

The octopus said: Eight arms are okay —
I can use each one in a different way!

With Number One
I eat a big cream bun —
ONE!

With Number Two
I hold a snooker cue —
ONE, TWO!

With Number Three
I can swing from a tree —
ONE, TWO, THREE!

With Number Four
I can paint the floor —
ONE, TWO, THREE, FOUR!

With Number Five
I can take a drive —
ONE, TWO, THREE, FOUR, FIVE!

With Number Six
I do conjuring tricks –
ONE, TWO, THREE, FOUR, FIVE, SIX!

With Number Seven
I draw a map of Devon –
ONE, TWO, THREE, FOUR, FIVE, SIX, SEVEN!

With Number Eight
I will open the gate –
ONE, TWO, THREE, FOUR, FIVE, SIX, SEVEN, EIGHT!

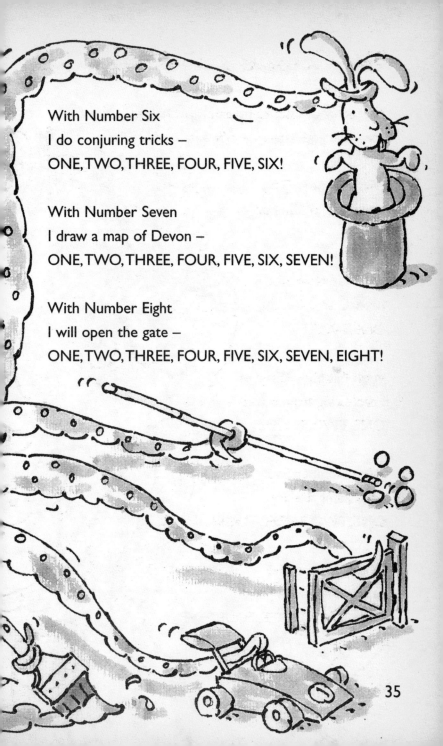

The Snow Goose's Limerick

A snow goose cried, flying through a blizzard:
"How I'd love all the skills of a wizard.
    I'm too cold in this spot,
    So I'd fly somewhere hot
And turn myself into a lizard!"

The Zebra's Joke

The zebra's really quite a sight:
His head is high, his mane is tossing.
The road is painted black and white
And there's the zebra, crossing!

The Bat on the Mat

The bat flew swiftly down the road
To make a visit to the toad.

"Bat, Bat,
What are you at,
Standing there on the Welcome Mat?"
"Though I begin
To bow and grin,
Nobody asks me to come right in."

"Bat, Bat,
Now why is that?"
"They think I'm a Vampire on the mat
And I'll fly and flounce
Like one of those Counts
Come to drink their blood in huge amounts."

"Bat, Bat,
No surprise in that,
For everyone knows what Dracula's at."
"From this Batmania
I must restrain ya –
I was never ever in Transylvania!"

"Bat, Bat,
It's nice to chat,
But you can't come into my cosy flat."
*"My reputation's
Not my creation —
The Count and I are no relation."*

"Bat, Bat,
On the Welcome Mat,
Why don't you come in and have a chat?
I'm a toad long since
But I can't convince
That a kiss won't turn me into a prince!"

Scrambled Animals

There was magic and mystery in the air
When the creatures met for the Secret Games
And so nobody knew just who was there
They scrambled the letters in all their names.

The PHOPGRASSER jumped and the GALEE flew
While the YEKMON climbed to the NIBOR's nest.
The PANTELOE raced with the GARKANOO
And the hairy RILLAGO thumped his chest.

The GLUELAS raced with the RYEL birds,
The TORPARS squawked and the HEEPS were bleating.
Can you unscramble the mixed-up words
And discover who was at that meeting?

The Footballing Seal

A circus seal, though just a pup,
Could balance beach-balls on his nose.
For hours and hours he kept it up,
While all around, the cheers rose.

But secretly he had a dream
Which he had never once revealed:
To join the local football team
And be a star upon the field.

One evening he slipped away
And sneaked into the football ground.
Each time he saw some brilliant play
His flippers made a clapping sound.

One player fell and broke his arm,
One started putting in the boot;
He got sent off – then in alarm
The coach cried: "We've no substitute!"

The seal's big chance was now revealed!
He speedily obeyed the call
And up and down the football field
He slithered, balancing the ball.

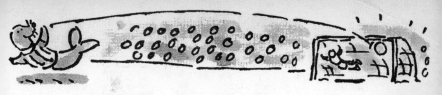

He flicked it deftly in the net –
Oh, how the home crowd did applaud!
And no one ever will forget
The magic of the goals he scored.

The coach then quickly signed him up
And soon their reputation rose –
And when the seal's team won the Cup
He balanced it upon his nose!

The Pelican's Trick

The pelican's enormous beak
With fishes he just loves to fill,
But finds that when he starts to speak,
Out of his open beak they spill.
So now that large and greedy bird
At last has come to understand
That if he wants to say a word
He has to write it in the sand.

The Hamster's Wheel

Hamster, running round your wheel,
You're keeping very busy.
Hamster, tell me how you feel?
I'm feeling very dizzy!

The Aardvark's Battle

The aardvark hasn't much claim to fame
In fact, he wouldn't be missed
Except that he's always the very first name
In the alphabetical list.

"I've got two A's, hooray, hooray!
And that gives me the crown!"
But another creature had thought of a way
To get the aardvark down.

The armadillo had dreamed a dream
When he laid his head on the pillow
That he'd added two A's, so his name would seem
To be spelt as AAARMADILLO.

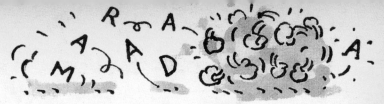

He woke and cried, "I've changed my name –
Now I'm at the very top!"
The aardvark said, "It's a crying shame
And this lark has got to stop!"

They had a battle that lasted for days
They were beaten black and blue
They tore bits off each other, including their A's
And other letters too.

In the end there were two small creatures there
That were never in any Ark
For all that was left of the battling pair
Were a DILLO and a VARK.

The Slug's Hope

Who believes the slimy slug
When he says he needs a hug?
In the basin!   Pull the plug!
Down he slithers, glug-glug-glug.

Who knows? – down there, his ugly mug
Might delight some other slug
And the slug will get his hug
Down where the waters glug-glug-glug.

The Ravens in the Tower

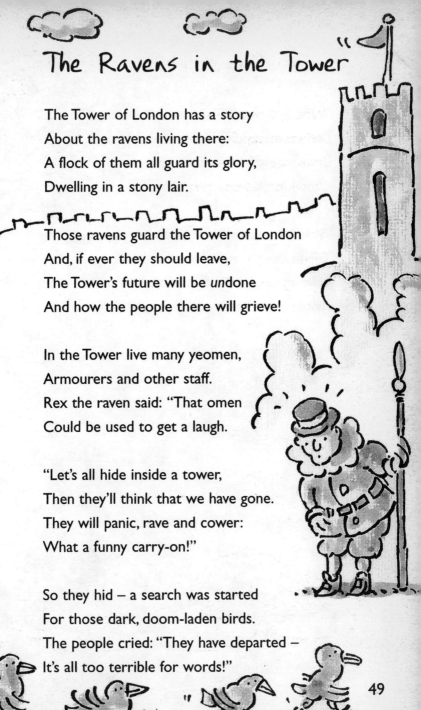

The Tower of London has a story
About the ravens living there:
A flock of them all guard its glory,
Dwelling in a stony lair.

Those ravens guard the Tower of London
And, if ever they should leave,
The Tower's future will be undone
And how the people there will grieve!

In the Tower live many yeomen,
Armourers and other staff.
Rex the raven said: "That omen
Could be used to get a laugh.

"Let's all hide inside a tower,
Then they'll think that we have gone.
They will panic, rave and cower:
What a funny carry-on!"

So they hid – a search was started
For those dark, doom-laden birds.
The people cried: "They have departed –
It's all too terrible for words!"

49

Disaster in the air they scented –
The yeomen flung their spears about.
Could the trouble be prevented
If the fire brigade came out?

Would the Crown Jewels be taken?
The ravens thought it quite a lark
To see the people all so shaken,
As they perched there in the dark.

Then they all heard midnight striking –
Suddenly a ghost appeared.
This wasn't to the ravens' liking –
In fact they found it very weird!

It was a queen whose head was chopped off
By the cruel king, right there.
Now she held the head he'd lopped off
Out before her, by the hair.

All the ravens started squawking,
Shrieked and flapped their wings about.
Round and round the ghost kept walking
Till the frightened birds flew out.

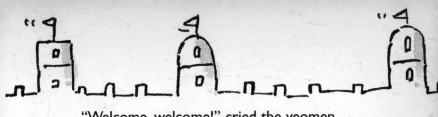

"Welcome, welcome!" cried the yeomen,
Stroking them with great relief.
The Tower was saved from fire and foemen –
Now it wouldn't come to grief.

The ravens' caws said: "We are staying!"
Though Rex's head turned grey with fright,
And no more tricks those birds are playing
In the middle of the night.

Let's all clap our fins and claws,
Our wings, our hooves, our furry paws!
Here next week in sun or rain
The Thursday Club will meet again.

Page 40: Scrambled Animals
GRASSHOPPER, EAGLE, MONKEY, ROBIN, ANTELOPE,
KANGAROO, GORILLA, SEAGULL, LYRE, PARROTS,
SHEEP

The Third Thursday

We're gathered for our Thursday meeting;
To one and all I give my greeting.

The skunk begins, so hold your nose!
The kookaburra strikes a pose.
We'll meet the shellfish and the pheasant,
A sheep who gets a woolly present.
There's snakes alive, and games to share,
A tortoise racing with a hare
And pigeons in Trafalgar Square
And last a lion who gets a scare!

Tell your story, tell your rhyme,
Come and tell it, now's the time.

The Skunk's Delight

The skunk said: "I've no idea why
Every creature I pass seems so shy.
 They snort and they sniff
 And they cry: 'What a whiff!'
Whenever I'm passing them by."

His friend said: "A skunk casts a spell
Which makes them feel very unwell.
 But don't take it bad
 If your scent drives them mad —
To *me* you smell perfectly swell!"

The Kookaburra's Laugh

In the silent Bush when the bright dawn broke
Up in a gum-tree the kookaburra woke
And he laughed and he laughed on his perch in the tree:
    HA-HA! HA-HA! HO-HO! HEE-HEE!

A wallaby said with a great big yawn:
"That kookaburra wakes me every dawn.
We must stop him laughing up there in his tree,
    HA-HA! HA-HA! HO-HO! HEE-HEE!"

The wallaby, the wombat and the cockatoo
Told him tearful stories till they all felt blue
But the kookaburra said: "No tears for *me*!
    HA-HA! HA-HA! HO-HO! HEE-HEE!"

So they all peeled onions before his face,
Played funeral music on a double-bass –
Said the kookaburra: "You won't sadden *me*!
    HA-HA! HA-HA! HO-HO! HEE-HEE!"

Along came a dingo, saying "G'day, you folks –
At last here's someone who'll laugh at my jokes!
The kookaburra's bound to laugh at *me* –
    HA-HA! HA-HA! HO-HO! HEE-HEE!"

His jokes were so bad that the kookaburra wept –
So the others hired the dingo to joke while they slept.
Now no more at dawn comes the laugh from the tree:
    "HA-HA! HA-HA! HO-HO! HEE-HEE!"

The Shellfish's Tongue Twister

The selfish shellfish shimmies to the sea.
"See me shimmy and shake," says she.
"The shops sell fish but they shan't sell me!"
Says the shimmying selfish shellfish!

The Pheasant's Grouse

The pheasant said: "Noble and Peasant
Are each going after the pheasant.
    Whenever we fly
    Their bullets whizz by –
It really is very unpleasant!"

The Sheep's Sweater

A sheep called Shirley
Got up early
When shearing day came round.
The shears went BUZZ
And her woolly fuzz
Fell round her on the ground.

There's three bags full
Of Shirley's wool –
No other sheep did better.
Now people sit
And knit and knit
To fashion many a sweater.

In green and blue
And scarlet too
They make a lovely sight
But Shirley's sad –
She wished she had
A sweater just as bright.

A girl called Dee
Had chanced to see
The look in Shirley's eyes.
She said: "I'll make
For Shirley's sake
A colourful surprise!"

With reds and blues
In rainbow hues
Dee's sweater glowed and
shone.
She went and kneeled
In Shirley's field
To help her put it on.

Oh, how that sheep
Would prance and leap
And roll upon the ground!
For, thanks to Dee,
She knows that she's
The best-dressed sheep around!

The Sssnakes' Hisss

A sssnake sssaid sssadly, "I confesss
I cannot ssstand the letter S!
Because we alwaysss ssspeak like thisss
They think all we can do is hisss!

And when we move, we sssnake around
Just like an S upon the ground.
Ssso let usss show that we can do
The shapes of other lettersss too."

The sssnakes made A and B and C
And F and M and X and E
And D and L and Y and T –
An alphabet for all to see.

The other creatures came to gape,
For none of them could change their shape.
They told the sssnakes: "We won't forget
You taught us all the alphabet!"

63

Animal Games

It's time now for more of the Animal Games –
We give you the clues and you find out the names!

My First shows the colours he has on his tail
My Second's forked tongue will bite without fail
My Third has long ears and goes hopping and hopping
My Fourth wakes up early and crows without stopping.
My Fifth loves the water and rapidly swims
My Sixth has a hard shell and very short limbs.

When you know them, then take the first letter of each
And put them together, the answer to reach.

The Tortoise And The Hare's Race

The tortoise plodded along the road
The shell she carried was a heavy load.
"Slowcoach! Slowcoach!" cried the hare,
"It will take you a year to get anywhere!

"But I am the fastest fellow alive
As swift as a swallow when it makes a dive
And just as nimble as a mountain goat is!"
The tortoise tried to take no notice.

The hare went on with his taunts and sneers
Till the tortoise said: "Listen, Floppy Ears –
You may think I move at a snail-like pace,
But I could beat you if we had a race."

"You're on!" said the hare with a laughing grin,
"If I race with you I'll be sure to win."
The other animals gathered round
And the hare set off with a leap and a bound.

A hundred metres along the track
The hare stopped running and took a look back.
Then he gave a bellow of scornful laughter
As the faraway tortoise plodded after.

Said the hare: "I'm certain to win the Cup,
So I'll just relax till she catches up."
He lay back then and soon he slept
While behind him the tortoise slowly crept.

An hour went by, until at last
The tortoise got there, and ambled past.
She shouted: "Now the victory's mine!"
As she walked across the finishing line.

The cheers of the crowd woke up the hare
And all he could do was stand and stare
As the tortoise said, with a grin on her face:
"It's SLOW AND STEADY that wins the race!"

The Pigeons' Perch

The pigeons in Trafalgar Square
Were watching Nelson's statue there.
One said: "That Admiral, you know –
His first name was Horatio,
And when against his foes he battled
His enemies were really rattled!"

The other pigeons said: "Your history
To us is nothing but a mystery.
While Nelson stands there looking solemn
We've other uses for his Column.
No longer do we need to search –
The Admiral makes a perfect perch!"

The Lion that Croaked

The jungle was quiet as the fresh dawn broke:
The jungle was quiet, till the lion woke!
He roared: "Who's King of the Jungle? WHO?"
And the other creatures cried: "YOU, YOU, YOU!"

But one fine day when the lion woke,
Nothing came out but a curious croak.
He moaned: "I am ill and my throat is sore,
And I can't make a sound when I try to roar."
The creatures, now they'd a chance to try it,
Rather enjoyed the peace and quiet.

But the lion feared what might be in store
If they once discovered he'd lost his roar –
Then King of the Jungle he'd be no more!
So the King of the Jungle tried cures galore...

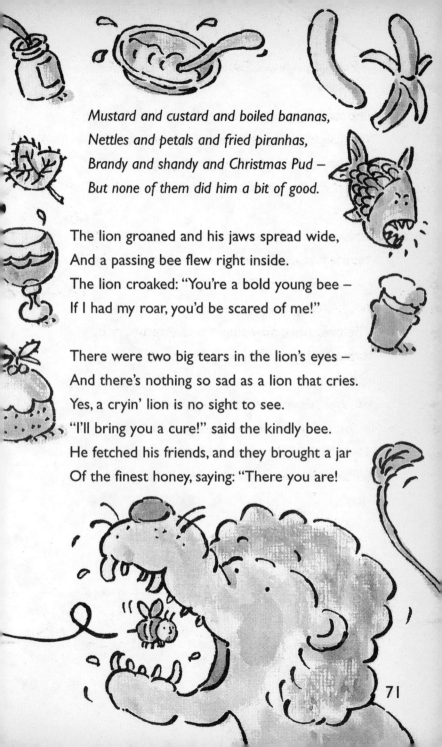

Mustard and custard and boiled bananas,
Nettles and petals and fried piranhas,
Brandy and shandy and Christmas Pud –
But none of them did him a bit of good.

The lion groaned and his jaws spread wide,
And a passing bee flew right inside.
The lion croaked: "You're a bold young bee –
If I had my roar, you'd be scared of me!"

There were two big tears in the lion's eyes –
And there's nothing so sad as a lion that cries.
Yes, a cryin' lion is no sight to see.
"I'll bring you a cure!" said the kindly bee.
He fetched his friends, and they brought a jar
Of the finest honey, saying: "There you are!

71

It's soothing and smoothing and rich and runny –
The purest of cures is surely honey.
Swallow and wallow and tell me true:
Aren't you feeling as good as new?"

The lion said: "Thank you, you've cured my cough."
"We are glad," said the bees – and they all buzzed off.

Next morning the lion woke up once more.
He opened his mouth and prepared to roar.
The bee flew in and said: "Don't you dare!
The jungle now has a peaceful air.
If you roar again, and get crusty and cross
And strut around like a bullying boss,
We'll be back to punish you, Jungle King –
We'll fly into your mouth and we'll sting, sting, sting!"
"Okay," said the lion, "but there's just one thing. . ."

He gazed at the bees, looking all forlorn:
"A lion must roar, that's the way we're born.
Roaring is just what a lion does,
Like a dove must coo, and a bee must buzz."
"That's true," said the bee, "and I can't deny it.
You can go on roaring – but keep it quiet!"

The jungle now is a quiet place.
As soon as the sun has shown his face,
The lion his leafy realm explores,
And the creatures smile as the lion roars
Ever so quietly....   Grrrrrr....
Ever so quietly....   Grrrrrr....

A soft, rich sound, that seems to please
The bees that buzz in the nearby trees...
Ever so quietly....   Bzzzzzz....
Ever so quietly....   Bzzzzzz....

Ever so quietly....   Grrrrrr....
Ever so quietly....   Grrrrrr....

Let's all clap our fins and claws,
Our wings, our hooves, our furry paws!
Here next week in sun or rain
The Thursday Club will meet again.

The Fourth Thursday

Now Thursday has come round once more
What stories do we have in store?

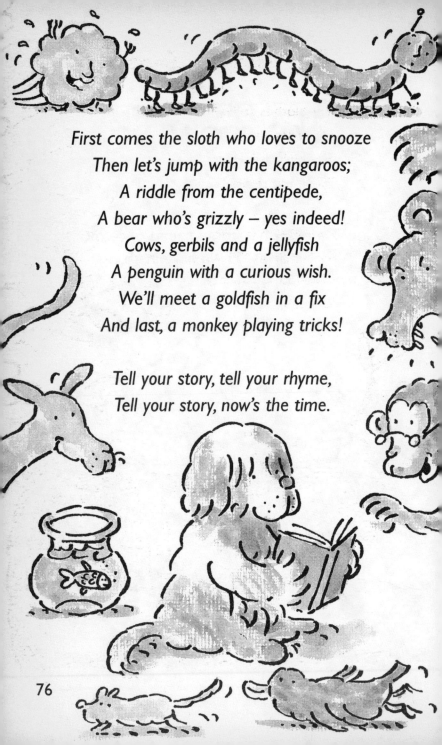

First comes the sloth who loves to snooze
Then let's jump with the kangaroos;
A riddle from the centipede,
A bear who's grizzly — yes indeed!
Cows, gerbils and a jellyfish
A penguin with a curious wish.
We'll meet a goldfish in a fix
And last, a monkey playing tricks!

Tell your story, tell your rhyme,
Tell your story, now's the time.

The Sloth's Snooze

The sloth is so lazy
He dozes all day
He thinks it is crazy
To go out to play.

He thinks it is crazy
To run, jump and crawl
The sloth is too lazy
To get up at all!

The Kangaroo's Jump

In Mother's pouch sits baby Joey
Safe and snug when winds are blowy.
But when his mother starts to jump
Young Joey's pouch goes bump, bump, bump!

He asks his mother, "Must I hide?
I'd really like to be outside."
"No, Joey, no! Don't be a fool –
You'll stay for months there, that's the rule."

One day when jumping through the bush
Joey decides to give a push.
Then up he flies, and with one bound
He finds he's landed on the ground.

His mother hops and hops again
Across the red Australian plain.
She doesn't know that Joey's out
And going on a walkabout!

Now Joey wonders what's in store:
This new wide world he must explore.
He says, "Adventure is my goal!"
And falls into a rabbit hole.

He clambers from that mucky place
And wind blows dust into his face.
An emu, feathery and fat,
Then nearly squashes Joey flat

A cockatoo who's passing through
Says, "I could make a meal of you !"
So Joey rolls into a ball
Hoping he won't be seen at all.

The furious wind now gives him grief
And sends him tumbling like a leaf.
He hits a thorn-bush, crying, "OUCH!" –
And wishes he could find his pouch.

Joey's in luck – his mother's here.
She says, "Jump in now, Joey dear.
You are a bad young kangaroo –
I don't know what we'll do with you!"

Now, when his mother hops and jumps
Young Joey doesn't mind the bumps.
He says, "The world is full of fear –
When I'm grown up, I'll stay right here!"

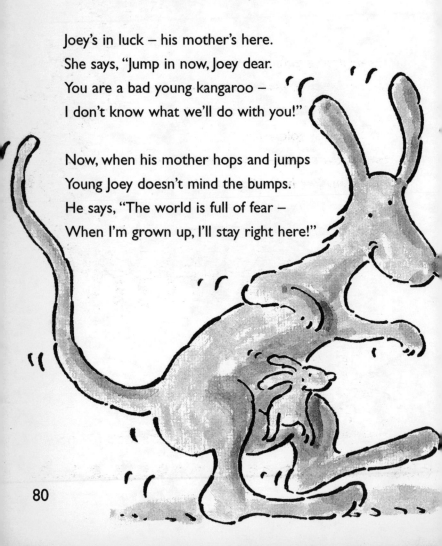

The Centipede's Riddle

"I've a hundred feet," said the centipede,
"So I put on my shoes at a very slow speed.
Now while I do,
Here's a riddle for YOU!"

The centipede took off eighty-two shoes,
And he put on seventeen brand-new shoes,
  Fourteen old shoes
  Seven gold shoes,
Twenty low shoes, twenty snow-shoes –
How many feet had still got no shoes?

The Grizzly Bear's Grizzle

The grizzly bear complained so busily,
No wonder that they called him Grizzly!
He grizzled when they talked of honey
And said it cost a lot of money.
When wake-up calls his nerves were grating
He shouted: "Quiet! I'm hibernating!"

One day they took him from his lair
Thinking he was a polar bear.
They brought him to the Arctic waste
Which really wasn't to his taste,
And so he grizzled more and more
Upon that bleak and icy shore.

A polar bear came up to him
And said: "Come on, let's have a swim!"
They plunged into the Arctic seas.
The grizzly said: "I'm going to freeze!
This climate's not what I would wish –
Besides, I have no taste for fish."

The polar bear said: "You're a pain –
We'll have to send you back again.
Compared to here, your homeland sizzles –
Go back and bore them with your grizzles!"

And so the grizzly bear went forth,
Abandoning the frozen North.
He doesn't grizzle any more –
But how his Polar stories bore!

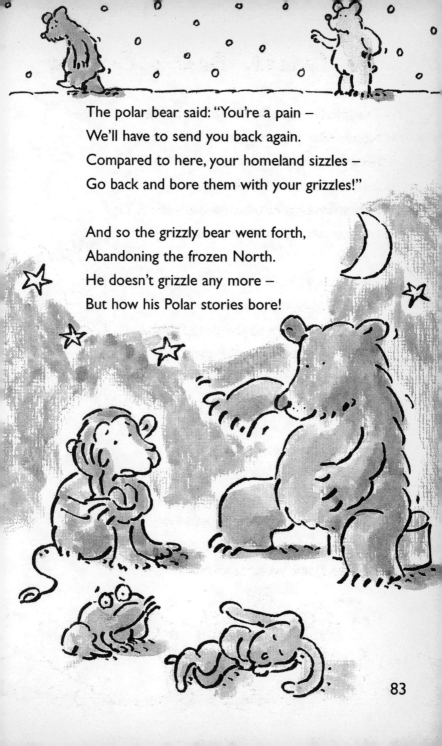

The Cow's Leap

Carrie the cow looked up at the sky
And watched the moon as it floated by.
She knew that once upon a time
According to a nursery rhyme
Which was a major childhood hit,
A cow like her jumped over it.

She said: "To show what I can do
I'm going to try and jump it too."
The other cows heard every word
And thought the notion quite absurd.
They raised their heads and laughed and laughed
And told her she was going daft.

Then Carrie in the moonlit night
Looked up, and knew that they were right.
She thought: "I'll show I'm not a fool –
The moon's reflected in that pool."
She told the others: "Watch me, please!"
And jumped across the pool with ease.

The moon was there, they must admit,
And Carrie had jumped over it.
So as the moon shone down its rays
The cows all gave a MOO of praise!

The Gerbil's Boast

"I'm a genius," boasted the gerbil,
"And my cleverest talents are verbal,
   So listen now, please,
    While I speak Japanese!"
But all that came out was a burble.

The Jellyfish's Tongue Twister

Jellyfish Bob
Is a wobbly blob
A wobbly blob is he.
He's a slobbery slob
With a gobbly gob
But Bob won't gobble ME!

The Penguin's Flight

Pippa the penguin wondered why
Though she was a bird, she couldn't fly.
She flapped her wings – it was all in vain:
She fell back down on the ice again.

Her mother told her to dry her tears:
"We haven't flown for a million years!
Why should we fly, when you know it's true
There's so many other things to do?

We can slip and slither and swim and slide,
And lie down flat on the ice and glide."
But Pippa still didn't think it fair
That she couldn't fly up there in the air.

A helicopter with fresh supplies
Came down on the cold Antarctic ice.
Pippa, though some might think her daft,
Hid on the runner below the craft.

The helicopter began to fly
And up went Pippa into the sky.
With her stubby wings she gripped her perch
As the chopper started to swoop and lurch.

She gazed with rapture down below
Upon that world of ice and snow,
Of mountain peak and frozen stream,
And saw the floating icebergs gleam.

She watched, upon the frozen rock,
Blank dots that moved – her penguin flock.
And much as Pippa loved to roam
She wondered how she'd get back home.

The helicopter swerved and tipped
And off the runner Pippa slipped.
Down, down she fell, into the water
And blessed the icy waves that caught her.

She swam to shore – her mother cried:
"Wherever did you go and hide?"
And Pippa said: "I took a flight
And saw the world from quite a height.
Some day I may fly even higher –
In fact, I'll be a Frequent Flyer!"

The Goldfish's Task

The cat said: "Goldfish, swimming in the water,
Each day you swim for a mile and a quarter,
Yet you never get anywhere – on the whole,
Is it worth all that swimming around your bowl?"

"Oh yes," said the goldfish, "don't you know, my friend,
That if I stopped swimming, the world would end?
The water would gush from my goldfish bowl
And over the Earth the floods would roll."

"Swim on," said the cat, "you're a gallant fish,
And the end of the world's not what I wish.
It's best to be cautious, though the risk is slight –
After all, friend goldfish, you might be right!"

The Bali Monkeys' Game

The monkeys in a Bali park
Thought up a very clever lark.
The visitors from many places
Wore spectacles upon their faces.

The monkeys pleased them with their poses,
Then snatched the glasses from their noses!
And though the people might complain
They wouldn't give them back again.

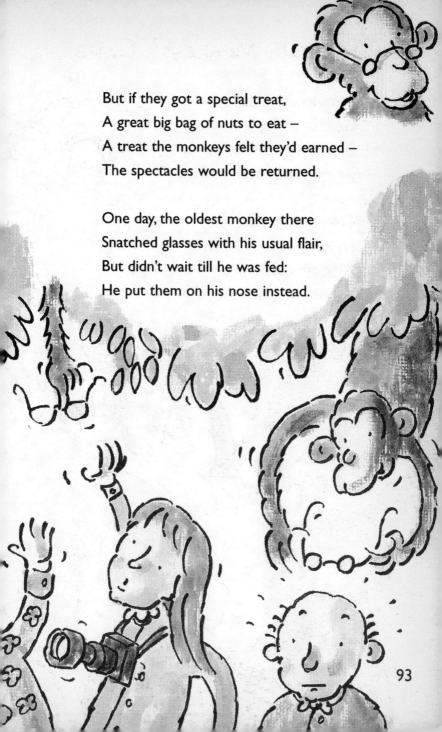

But if they got a special treat,
A great big bag of nuts to eat –
A treat the monkeys felt they'd earned –
The spectacles would be returned.

One day, the oldest monkey there
Snatched glasses with his usual flair,
But didn't wait till he was fed:
He put them on his nose instead.

He cried: "A miracle's occurred!
My sight was getting very blurred,
But now I've got these glasses here
My vision's once more sharp and clear."

The woman did her best to plead –
Brought nuts to tempt the monkey's greed;
But all her efforts were in vain:
He wouldn't give them back again.

So now, among the great delights
Of Bali's many tourist sights,
There's one that all the rest surpasses:
A laughing monkey, wearing glasses!

Storytelling Never Ends

Let's all clap our fins and claws,
Our wings, our hooves, our furry paws!
Here next week in sun or rain
The Thursday Club will meet again.
Storytelling never ends –
So till next Thursday, farewell friends!

Page 77: The Centipede's Riddle
FOUR

3 8002 00899 9684